Caricature of Sinclair Lewis by Carl Rose used in *Shake Well Before Using* by Bennett Cerf, Simon and Schuster, 1948. A member of the publisher's staff sent this advance copy to Lewis who labelled the male figure "George" and the female "Ida". "George" refers to George Bielby, the minister of the Williamstown, Massachusetts Congregational Church, with whom Lewis had a short association. "Ida" is the author Ida Compton. (Courtesy of Simon and Schuster)

Sinclair Lewis At Thorvale Farm

A Personal Memoir

Ida L. Compton

RUGGLES PUBLISHING COMPANY
Sarasota

Copyright 1988 Estate of Ida L. Compton
Lewis Letters copyright 1987 St. Cloud State University, Minnesota

All rights reserved including the right of reproduction
in whole or in part in any form.

Library of Congress Catalog Number 88-092777
ISBN — 0915909-01-4

Design by Laura L. Nielsen
Composition by Lubin Typesetting, Sarasota, FL

Ruggles Publishing Company
960 Pomelo Avenue
Sarasota, Florida 34236

"First Printing"

I

In 1951 telephone dials had not yet replaced operators in the Berkshire Hills of Massachusetts where I made my home. I always knew by the extended ring that a long distance call was coming in. I liked knowing, it gave me a moment to prepare for something of possible significance.

When the bell rang, long and persistently, early one January morning, I wondered who might be phoning me from more than five miles away. To my preoccupied, "Hello," the operator replied, "St. Cloud, Minnesota, is calling."

"Hello, this is Claude. I say, this is Claude," a chipper male voice came through clearly. "Hal's ashes arrived yesterday. I say, Hal's ashes arrived yesterday. They came by plane from Rome to New York. The memorial services are Sunday, this Sunday. Helen and I want you to come out to be with us; come out to be with us."

How irritated his brother Hal would have been with Claude's characteristic rhythmic repetition. "Hell, why can't he say something just once and let it go at that?" he would say.

"Claude, I'm sorry but I don't think I can make it," I answered, after some hesitation. "We'll meet you in Minneapolis at the airport, at the airport," Claude continued, ignoring my reply. "Wire me the time. I say, wire me the time and the flight when you know. Better leave today. It's 30 below here, and a blizzard on the way."

"I'll let you know Claude. Sorry that I'm not sure."

"Hal's ashes" were the remains of Sinclair Lewis, the first American to win the Nobel Prize in Literature. Lewis had died two weeks before, in Rome. The remains of the creator of Babbitt, Elmer Gantry, Arrowsmith and Dodsworth had arrived back home. The epilogue to his life was to take place on Sunday, January 28 in Sauk Centre, Minnesota, where he was born. His brother, Dr. Claude Lewis, now calling me, was in charge of the arrangements. I had come to know Claude very well in the course of his visits to his brother. Only a year or so earlier I had asked him to come East when Sinclair Lewis seemed bent on destroying himself with drink. Without hesitation or question he came. I realized that I must go to be with him now.

The bouncy gaiety of Claude's telephone call had, at first, been slightly irritating, but I should have remembered that this was part of his general manner. For Claude everything was to be enjoyed. Nothing in his life was tinged with the constant "angst" experienced by his brother Hal. Years later I learned that Claude had faced death with the same verve and sense of excitement. His attitude was not the result of innocence since he was for many years a well recognized physician in Minnesota.

Four hours later, after exploring the various travel possibilities, I was sitting in the club car of a train steaming westward. While I waited for a scotch and soda I took note of two wardrobes, the one I had with me and the one I had left behind, wishing I could make a few quick changes. Lewis would have blurted out "Damn woman! Death, burial or a helluva weather mess and what does she worry about? What she puts on her back!"

"Thirty below zero" Claude had warned "and a blizzard on the way." And I had nothing to cover my meager leather pumps. I smiled as I thought of how my overlooking the proper attire would also have irritated Lewis. Except during his drinking bouts Sinclair Lewis was very cautious about his health and prepared at all times for bodily discomforts.

As the ice in my glass slithered with the sway of the train, I felt a deep sadness that his life, which was filled with great accomplishment and worldwide fame, had ended in an untimely death, but not before his outstanding successes had been mixed with failures and controversies. Despite the acclaim, Lewis was in fact a lonely person and I, who had known him for only four years, would be one of a very few who would feel a sense of loss and mourning.

My first meeting with Sinclair Lewis was quite by chance. It was in June, 1947. He was living on his estate, Thorvale Farm, outside of Williamstown, Massachusetts, and had just completed his twentieth book, "Kingsblood Royal."* The book had received mixed reviews, some unfavorable, many lukewarm. But the literary world had been reminded that Sinclair Lewis was still a force to be reckoned with. At the time I was a graduate student at Williams College and helping to manage the bookstore in town. I had just started writing book reviews for the local newspapers and Lewis had read about my enthusiastic discussions of "Kingsblood Royal." Through Barnaby Conrad, then Lewis' secretary-companion and later a very successful author in his own right, I was invited to Thorvale for dinner to meet the great man himself.

Lewis had been living in Williamstown for a little over a year, but the town had seen very little of him. Rumor had it that he chose to be isolated, that he had no desire to meet anyone locally and that he wanted complete privacy to work and time

---

* A complete list of Sinclair Lewis' books is included in a condensed outline biography at the end.

to entertain his famous friends from out of town. Consequently the invitation to be his guest came as an exciting surprise. It also brought on some apprehension. I had read about his idiosyncrasies and decided that I should be on the alert for almost anything. Moreover, I, who ordinarily had no trouble talking, feared that I would become tongue-tied.

The house at Thorvale Farm was a lovely white, New England shingled type, surrounded by 660 rolling acres, which looked across a valley towards Mount Greylock a few miles distant. It was the last of a series of homes Lewis had devoted many years of his life and many dollars of his income to acquiring and abandoning. The estate had a tennis court, a caretaker's cottage and a swimming pool with bathhouses tucked away in a charming grove of birch trees. A bubbling brook wound through the grounds and Lewis had supervised the building of outdoor picnic facilities in two singularly scenic locations on its banks. At one time he also owned a farm with livestock which a tenant farmer supervised.

On the arranged afternoon I walked up on the side terrace of the house and found that I had interrupted a game of chess between Barnaby and a young lady houseguest. After a casual and relaxed introduction, Barnaby said that Lewis was upstairs dressing and would be right down. I then became absorbed in their chess game and didn't notice when Lewis arrived at the screen door which led onto the terrace. "Oh, so you're Ida!" he said, as he swung the door open. He was wearing a baggy tweed suit over his tall, thin frame, and dark horn-rimmed glasses, which attracted attention to his face above the collar of a white shirt. As he stepped onto the porch he reached out to me saying, "Now, come around on this side of the house and tell me about yourself." I jumped up like a puppet whose strings had been pulled.

"Barnaby came back from town yesterday with glowing reports of his meeting with you," he said, as we walked along.

And then after a pause, "Call me Red."

"Now come sit down" he said as he indicated a chair next to him. He spoke in a high pitched, clipped manner and turned toward me with a straightforward stare from compulsive blue eyes. His questions came in rapid fire order "Who are you?"; "Where did you come from?"; "Where were you educated?" I found myself being a little disappointed at the inquisition. But I was to learn later that this famous author, a world traveler and center of many social and intellectual gatherings, was shy and felt socially uncomfortable until some kind of rapport was established with those whom he was meeting for the first time.

I gave Lewis only as much information as I felt would give us some common meeting ground. He appeared especially interested in my pursuit of sports and dancing, neither of which, I learned later, he had ever indulged in, mostly because of his complete lack of coordination.

As the evening progressed Lewis continued to be in great form: voluble, amusing and charming. There wasn't any suggestion of formality. He was far easier to be with than most strangers. There was no hint of the loneliness which was so much a part of his life at the time.

It wasn't until later reflection that I realized that physically the man could be called ugly. His face was like a mask, badly pitted from frequent skin operations; his head was small for his over six foot gangling frame; his extremely long, skeletal hands protruded from his jacket sleeves and seemed to operate independently from his body. But he used them effectively and they were fascinating to watch.

At the end of the evening I was invited to return the next day for a swim in his pool "If you don't mind the very cold water." I had no idea that this would be the beginning of a close friendship.

To his brother Claude, and to everyone else in Minnesota, Harry Sinclair Lewis was known as "Hal". As an author he had dropped the first name. In the East and in Europe those who felt free to call him something more personal than "Mr. Lewis" knew him as "Red", a nickname he promoted even though the last trace of red had faded from his hair. There was something incongruous about this. At least a year passed before I came by it naturally; and then only after I had pieced together a reason for his delight in the name. There is something that smacks of "one of the boys" in "Red", an informality and "hail fellow well met" connotation. All this filled a need which he would usually deny vigorously, but acknowledged humorously in more candid moments.

I knew, as much as anyone can know about another person's unspoken thoughts, that talk of death was "verboten" with Lewis. In the years that I knew him I never heard him talk about dying. I happened to be with him shortly after he had learned of the passing of his close friend, Carl Van Doren, the successful historian and biographer. As if he had drawn a curtain and stepped in front of it to make the announcement, he said, "Carl died last month. Did you read about it?" Some note in his voice and the look in his eye stopped me from saying anything more than, "Yes."

If Lewis had lived to fulfill only half of his plans for the future, he would have been way past the age of the 86 years he predicted in his auto-obituary, *The Death of Arrowsmith* which was published in 1941. "His plans for so many years ahead impress me as being a pseudo-guarantee of living that long," Carl Van Doren once said in answer to my query about the seriousness of Lewis' constant projection into the future. "He seems to have a compulsion to communicate his intention for a long life; maybe he feels that if he has something definite to do, he will live the number of years it will take to do it."

When Lewis left for Europe in the fall of 1949 he had been in fair health. But in August of the next year, when I spent a week with him in Zurich, he showed definite signs of poor

This essay was assembled from notes, lectures, book reviews and other writings about Sinclair Lewis which Ida wrote over a period of many years. Unfortunately only a small portion of the account which she was writing at the time of her illness was sufficiently complete to be incorporated. But the essay will serve to illuminate the friendship between "Red" Lewis and Ida during the last years of his life.

health, although the old fire that had made him the artist he was still flared intermittently. Only three letters came from him after my return home. These were followed during the early winter by messages from Claude, each of which added to my own conviction that he was gravely ill. Lewis had asked me to assist in the selling of Thorvale and supervise the packing of his books and some mementos. I had anticipated detailed inquiries concerning my progress. Always an amateur inventory expert, he would want to know the kind of boxes used, what was in each, and what precaution had been taken against mildew and other spoilage. He was not a collector of mementos or "sentimental garbage" as he would say, but he had a few trinkets he prized: bits of statuary from the ruins of Pompeii, a crucifix which he had used when he acted in the play *Death Comes to the Archbishop,* and a cigarette box from Florence. The inquiries never came.

At one time word of death's call was spread with some degree of dignity and consideration. Today radio and television blare it into every tavern, filling station and beauty parlor as well as into the homes of those who are closest to the deceased. Thus I learned of Lewis' death on the morning of January 10; so I learned later, had Claude. One is never prepared for death, whenever it may strike, although certainly there is nothing quite so inevitable. And never have I found reason to question the thought that when a person dies a little bit of everyone he knew or touched dies with him.

The morning after my departure the train was in Chicago, which made Minnesota sound quite near. I called the airport from the station and made a reservation to Minneapolis, and then called St. Cloud. Claude's wife, Helen, answered with a warm advance greeting and warned that I might be delayed in Minneapolis because the all-night blizzard had blocked all the highways. Claude got on the phone and suggested that I try to catch the bus out of Minneapolis as soon as I arrived at the airport.

The whole Chicago area was moving laboriously under a thick blanket of snow. Twice our DC-6 taxied down the runway but we remained earthbound, returning once to drop Milwaukee passengers, after receiving word that the Milwaukee airport was not safe for incoming planes. Our plane reported back to the ramp the second time to wait for a report from our next airport, Madison. While waiting, the sleety drizzle landing on the metal surface coated the fuselage with ice. Huddled in blankets provided by the stewardess, we waited while our flying igloo was defrosted.

I found myself thinking once more about this sudden journey. I could almost hear Lewis' words, "Don't spend your money foolishly, Ida. You don't want to go to that damn silly memorial service. Too much else to see in this world that's alive. It's a long trip just to watch my ashes being poured into the ground." But underneath I knew a part of him, the sentimental part he showed on rare occasions, would say, "God bless you, darling, I'm glad you'll be there."

The plane eventually became airborne and soared over the flat, snow covered Middle West, sparkling in its whiteness. This was the magnificent expanse of rich farm lands, unbroken by the ripple of a hill, described by Lewis with nostalgic enthusiasm. But then I also recalled how very much he had loved the hills of New England. He would sit for hours on his terrace at Thorvale looking at the valley below and across to the mountains. "Ida, you can travel the world over and find nothing that can rival this view," Lewis often remarked. "There's always something new to see."

Not one inch of the miles we covered between Chicago and Minneapolis had escaped the blizzard. Weather had been a major concern in all of Claude's letters since Thanksgiving, second only to news of Lewis. "Winter hit us yesterday, now five inches of snow and ten degrees above zero. Right now we are at the tail end of a 48-hour snowstorm and 20 below is predicted for tomorrow morning." Until my arrival I hadn't grasped the full meaning of his weather reports. Now I knew what 20 below felt like. When I walked from the plane to the waiting room I suffered a quick freeze and I stayed frozen for the rest of the trip. I didn't even notice the drop to 30 below when it came scarcely 24 hours later.

The conversation of the cab driver as he sped me through the snowy streets of Minneapolis made me aware of the quality Lewis had later longed for in his characteristically reserved New England confreres. In a completely disarming way the cab driver learned where I was from, where I was going, and he might have gathered a thumbnail biography if I hadn't countered with a few questions of my own. He was apologetic about the section of the city we were passing through because it was not the best part to represent Minneapolis. I believe that he would have given me a grand tour of the town at his own expense if I hadn't insisted that I was rushed. He showed concern about the bus trip on the next lap of my trip, hoping that the roads would be open. One more ticket, one more mode of travel, and I would be at Claude's.

The highway to St. Cloud was like one of those straight lines I had seen from the air, with snow heaped into wall-like embankments on both sides. With the view obscured to left and right, we rode along in a trench of snow. Travel weary and numb with cold, suspended between memories of Red and anticipation of the memorial services tomorrow, I leaned back in the seat and closed my eyes.

Claude was waiting for me at the bus station. He was a ruddy-faced, medium height man, whose sparkling blue eyes and still-red hair identified him at once as Sinclair Lewis' brother. His eyes darted and gleamed, but never with Red's driven look. His voice was lively and sharp, with no mysterious inflections. He had little concern with what might have been, could be, or should be, but only with what is. "There you are! Are you frozen?" His arm going around my shoulder provided some welcome warmth. "Sure glad you came. I told you the ashes arrived from Rome. Nice program planned for tomorrow. Lots of things I want to talk to you about. You know, Harry Maule called me and asked me to reserve a room for him in a hotel in Sauk Centre." And he laughed his high, short laugh. "If he ever saw that Sauk Centre Hotel, he'd never ask to stay there! It's been the same for the last fifty years. He's going to stay with us, and Michael, too." Harry Maule was Lewis' devoted friend who guided his manuscripts through Random House, publisher of all of his recent novels. Michael was Lewis' only living son, whose mother was Dorothy Thompson.

I didn't try to see out of the heavily frosted windows but listened to Claude describing the storm, the fast-dropping temperature, and the details of the precautions he had taken at home to keep out the cold. It apparently was a family trait, this preparedness, this farsightedness for every contingency. Lewis had it, too, with amusing overtones. I was completely overwhelmed the first time he showed me the spare deep freeze unit in the basement at Thorvale. He explained that in case of an unusual snowstorm, sickness or other unforeseen emergency, the freezer in the basement would hold enough food for at least six months. Although Lewis neither swam, played tennis nor croquet and few of his guests indulged in these sports, he had an excellent tennis court and kept on hand two new rackets, with three sealed cans of balls. The swimming pool was carefully cleaned, the bathhouses were always in readiness and several rubber tubes and floats were available. Two croquet sets had never been removed from their boxes.

Helen had been excitedly awaiting the arrival of her "Eastern" guests. She showed me to my room immediately, and suggested a hot bath. Later, downstairs, after first peering into the kitchen and offering to help Helen who was fixing the pheasant she and Claude had shot the previous fall, I joined Claude in the front room where he was buried deep in the evening papers. Removing the cigar from his mouth, he pointed to some newspaper articles about his brother. Lewis had never interrupted his late afternoon ritual of reading the news for a friend. He always motioned to a chair and continued reading until he was through. Claude went right on in the same way.

Although I had written Claude in detail of my visit with Lewis in Switzerland the previous summer, he asked me to review everything I could remember. Claude recalled that the four months he had spent with his brother in Europe the previous year were memorable.

"You know, Ida, everyone knew Hal and we never went anywhere but someone didn't recognize him and then the invitations would begin. He got me a private audience with the Pope. I didn't know what to expect until I found myself in a little room with only three people and pretty soon the Pope came in. I was third in line. We had a nice conversation. He asked about Hal right off. Knew him well and had read most of his books. And then I told him about doctoring in St. Cloud up here at the Catholic Hospital and he knew all about that from some of the priests there. It was easy talking to him." Claude was interrupted by the arrival of Harry Maule and Michael Lewis.

After greeting the late-comers I joined Helen in the kitchen. I sauteed the almonds for the pheasant, removed the paraffin from the many jars of pickled watermelon, relish, preserves and gherkins, unmolded the sour cream vegetable salads and placed the home-made deep-frozen sweet rolls in the oven. Everything was a little special. "Fixing dinner" was routine for Helen, but "feeding three hungry men", two of them company, was a third degree rite.

When Helen had checked everything twice, she called to Claude saying "the kitchen is ready", and we met in the dining room for dinner. I sat next to Michael, realizing as he talked of England, the drama, his love for the theatre and his observations on the "barbarianism" of some American ways that he was completely alien to his father's origin. Physically he resembled what I imagine Lewis had looked like at the same age. Like his father, he was driven by a restless impatience and nervous energy. Because of his extended stay in London and recent return to New York, he seemed to be a person of no time and place, a composite of insecurity camouflaged with conceit. He had been in Rome for Christmas and told of his last visit with his father with no more obvious emotion than an indifferent child reciting a well-memorized Memorial Day piece.

We discussed Alec Manson, Lewis's last secretary. Michael thought he was a "tremendous chap"; Claude, who had traveled up to the Riviera and about France with him for two weeks, seemed to think he was a "good fellow". To me, Alec Manson was a perfect example of Lewis' ineptitude in appraising people. Lewis was inclined to attribute characteristics to individuals which they actually did not have, but which they could have been assigned-if he were writing about them in a novel. He saw what he wanted and imagined the rest. Consequently he rarely knew anyone or even came close to knowing anyone. He was too preoccupied with fictionalizing them.

Alexander Manson had entered Lewis' life in 1950 when Lewis went to Europe for the last time and settled down in Florence to rewrite what was eventually published as *World So Wide*. There was a quite well-known colony of Americans in Florence, well-to-do cosmopolitans drawn together mostly by mutual interests in arts and letters. There are frequently "hangers-on" in such communities, more or less professional, polished and intellectual, but who are attempting to live on a higher financial plane than they could sustain with their own resources.

Alec Manson seemed to me to be one of these. He was the

son of an English father and a Polish mother and had been educated in Switzerland's finest schools. He said that he had started at Oxford but left when World War II broke out to join the intelligence section of the British Army.

Alec attached himself to Lewis, made himself indispensable as a combination secretary, chauffeur, handy man and companion. Lewis liked him and sang his praises as one of the greatest finds of his life. In all of his letters to me before my visit to Europe the preceding summer, I had heard nothing but rave reports. In February he had written to me "Alexander Manson is the only good secretary I ever had, and I hope to God he'll stay with me the rest of my life. In efficiency — in intelligence and amusingness — he makes the others looks like dolts."

But Lewis' friends in Florence had become suspicious of Alec. Bernard Berenson, the internationally famous art critic who was a close friend of Lewis, was one of the leading figures in the American group there. Through Lewis I visited him while I was in Florence. Many of those I met during my visit, knowing I was a close friend of Lewis, felt free to let me know that they suspected Alec's motives to be largely mercenary. Lewis had so stubbornly refused to listen to their warnings that his relations with them had become strained. I was delegated to try to make Lewis see the situation when I visited him in Switzerland later in the month.

My visit with Lewis, Alec and the woman whom he introduced as his wife, Tina Lazzerini, underscored everything that had been reported to me by Berenson and others. But I found that it was useless to try to convince Lewis. Once he had made up his mind about a person it was impossible for a third person to convince him otherwise.

As Lewis continued on his way to drinking himself to death he became increasingly dependent on Alec. Alec was the principal person in charge of Lewis' controversial medical attention at the time of his death. Afterwards he unsuccessfully attempted to present himself to the Lewis estate executors as an heir. But that, of course, was to happen after the memorial service, and was not known to us as we sat conversing around Claude and Helen's dinner table.

By the next morning the temperature had fallen almost to 40 below as Claude had predicted, but the sun was shining brilliantly on the snow. After a ride around town we returned to thaw out and meet Isabel and Bob Agrell, Claude's daughter and her husband, who had driven up from Minneapolis.

As we left for Sauk Centre, Claude insisted that Harry Maule wear some black zippered galoshes, adding "I say, Mr. Maule, you take those right along with you back to New York. You can't get them like that there."

After we were seated in his car he told us, "Now between here and Sauk Centre there's not much to see; no, not much to see. Flat and straight all the way. I say, flat and straight all the way. Seventy-five percent of the people are of Scandinavian and German descent. Make good, honest, hard-working citizens, they do."

As the car sped along the cleared highway Claude explained, "Got wonderful equipment here for clearing snow. There, look over there! Those fellows got all that snow off here since yesterday." Claude's high pitched voice, muffled by the fur collar of his black coat, reached Michael and me in the back seat as we tried vainly to see out of the ice-coated windows.

"I remember traveling these country roads with a horse and buggy. After a storm like yesterday's I was lucky to cover three miles an hour."

"Here we come! There's the sign."

Ahead of us on the right of the road we managed to see a large white marker with red lettering reading:

WELCOME TO THE
ORIGINAL MAIN STREET
SAUK CENTRE
BUTTER CAPITAL OF THE WORLD

Harry Maule commented on "Centre" being spelled with an "re" which is chiefly the English way of spelling. And Michael spoke an aside to me about "of the world" — not "of the state" or "the country" but "of the world."

"Sauk Centre is a town of a few thousand," Claude continued, "in a region of wheat, corn, dairies and little groves, and a good many miles from that big city, Minneapolis, over there somewhere."

We were at the beginning of Main Street. "There's the library. Yup, same building was there when we were kids. That's the old Perkins drug store. My father had his office right upstairs in the back. I say, my father's office was right upstairs. That's the old Bank Building."

Claude didn't have to point out the theatre with its sign in bold letters "Main Street" in front of which Sinclair Lewis had his last picture taken in his hometown in 1947.

"I'll show you around before we go to the High School. There's the Episcopal Church, and that's the Gopher State Hatchery. Around the corner here is Third Street. My brother Fred's son works in that grocery store and lives at home with his mother. Fred died a few years back, you know."

As we rounded the corner with the street sign saying "Third Street", Claude's voice reached a higher pitch. "Now right up here in that white shingled house, 811 Third Street it is, is where Hal and I were born. After our mother died our father married again and we moved right across the street to that gray house. Hal was only seven then. Back over there is the stream we used to fish in."

Harry Maule asked, "Did Hal ever fish?"

"No, Hal was younger. He didn't pal with me much. If you

cut across the fields, there's a wonderful place to hunt birds. Yup, we had it all right in our backyard."

Helen reminded Claude that the services were scheduled for two-thirty and couldn't begin until we had arrived. "That's about all there is to see, anyway," Claude said with a little laugh. "We'll go along now to the High School."

Lewis had wanted there to be no religion associated with his burial. I had wondered what could be said and done at a memorial service that was not to be a memorial service in the accepted sense. Although the two words do not necessarily have a connection with religion, they call to mind church and prayer just as angels evoke a picture of heaven.

The starkness of the bare stage was relieved only by one basket of white flowers sent by Michael, and a black ribbon which draped the rostrum, a tribute from Lewis' editor in Rome. No echoes of the phenomenal international success of *Main Street* and *Babbitt* bounced from the walls; no applause for a Nobel Prize winner resounded there. Of the 500 or so Sauk Centre citizens who filled the darkened auditorium not one had intimately known Harry Sinclair Lewis. A handful of people who had come close to him occupied part of the front row; his brother and his wife, his son, his niece and her husband, Harry Maule and myself. Lewis had died in Rome among strangers and he was coming home to only a very few friends.

The simplicity and honesty of the services were very moving. Lewis frequently admitted his love for the theatre and his secret passion to act but he readily confessed that he never got beyond a grade C as a ham actor. Here in the final show he had top billing. Instead of the reporters who were somewhere in the back of the auditorium, I felt there should have been drama critics, fifth row center. The highest tribute of all was the omission of applause.

There was nothing labored in Laurel Kells' story of Lewis' youth. Kells had been a boyhood friend of Lewis, and he was now an attorney in his home town. He talked about Lewis and his early inclination toward books, reading everything in his reach, and then "living the characters of his reading." Often his friends found "they were talking not to Hal Lewis but to Sherlock Holmes, Napoleon, Robin Hood or some other hero." He developed an ability to concentrate which made it possible for him to do two things at one time, "one of those things was always reading." Lewis' high school graduating class had nine people, "but", said Kells, "so many people now claim to have graduated with him, the class roster has swelled like the passenger list of the Mayflower."

Laurel Kells walked back to the wings of the stage from which he had entered. The silence which followed engendered reflection. Lewis in Sauk Centre as Hal; Lewis before he had opened Pandora's box and before he had poured out *Main Street.* Then, without introduction we were listening to a reading of *The Long Arm of the Small Town.* Lewis had sent this piece to the youth of Sauk Centre in 1931, on the fiftieth anniversary of the high school annual, the "O-Sa-Ge." If in *Main Street* he had cut and probed, he had written this to say, I hurt to make you well, out of love. The citizens of Sauk Centre, long since having forgotten his scalpel and their indignation, had chosen the following words of the author as a farewell.

"It is extraordinary how deep is the impression made by the place of one's birth and rearing and how lasting are its memories. I find myself thinking of its streets and its people and the familiar, friendly faces when I am on the great avenues of New York, Paris, Berlin or Stockholm. I haven't the slightest regret that I was born and reared in a prairie village instead of in New England or New York, or old England or the continent of Europe. If I seem to have criticized the prairie villages, I have certainly criticized them no more than I have New York, Paris or the great universities. I am quite certain that I could have been born and reared no place in the world where I would have had more friendliness. It was a good time, a good place, and a good preparation for life."

Frederick Manfred, one of the many writers Lewis had helped in their beginning years, then analyzed Lewis' two visions: "the way things ought to be and the way things are." I recalled Lewis' remark, "An individual is as many different people as the number of people who know him." I wondered when all the paradoxical, enigmatic pieces of the jig saw puzzle he had been would be brought together, if ever.

In the bitter cold, snow covered Greenwood cemetery, out among the fields but less than a mile from Main Street, Claude clipped the green ribbon on the silver urn that held his brother's ashes. His gloved hand fumbled with the cover; he lifted the top and bent quickly to pour the ashes into the grave. Even here, there was nothing funereal. If anyone was sad, there were no tears to show it. Stepping back from the edge of the grave, Claude said, "Let's say the Lord's Prayer, quickly." With hands pressed to half-frozen ears some said it more quickly than others, and the Lord's Prayer echoed like an English round into eternity.

"The whole thing was good; I say, the whole thing was good," Claude observed in his usual clipped, cheery tone as soon as we had settled in his car. "That hot coffee down there at the high school will taste mighty good."

II

Lewis would be both furious and pleased if he knew that I was writing about him. I can hear him in his high-pitched voice saying, "Thank heavens, Ida, I can count on you. You'll never record every word I've ever spoken or every detail of my life." Yet at another time, in a half inebriated state, he practically dictated to me the beginnings of an autobiography, saying "No damn fool will get at me first."

Lewis was a man of marked opposites. He held in contempt anyone who could not take criticism; yet he became incensed at the slightest suggestion of criticism of himself. He laughed sympathetically at the set, rutted life of provincial Americans, holding that New Yorkers were the most provincial of all. Yet wherever he went in America, England or Europe he took with him his unbroken daily habits of living: coffee, prepared the night before and left in a thermos, to drink at five or six in the morning when he awoke; American cigarettes in an endless chain; his own typewriter and writing materials.

When playing chess he had great impatience with a partner who spent time planning the next move and didn't hesitate to show his annoyance. Yet he, himself, would sit for many minutes pondering on the most advisable maneuver. After one of his good humored but serious outbursts of impatience when I had hesitated, I remarked "I'd like to be able to figure you out!" We finished the game in silence. Then, like the information he catalogued in his mind for future reference, he pulled out my exclamation to examine it.

"Ida, you're as bad as all those phonies in psychiatry and psychology. You can't figure people out. Accept them! You can't say anything that will cause people to do certain things. Take these new avant garde writers indulging in a whim. Hhhmmm. Psychological novels! Four letter words, sex and psychology. People are people! Always have been. It's a lot of nonsense. In Germany after my first divorce I went to see a psychiatrist. I went once. I went on a walking tour all over Germany instead of going back. Did me more good than telling someone about my childhood."

It was quite apparent that Lewis was not sold on psychiatry. But months later Norman Mailer and his wife came to visit him, and an interesting evening it was. *The Naked and The Dead* was raging in popularity much as *Main Street* had in its day. Mailer was of the new, violent school of writers and was telling us about his theories of developing characters, every bit of it based on different concepts of psychology. Lewis, not out of politeness, because he never bothered with social graces or intellectual compromises, agreed completely with Mailer, even enlarging on the thesis and showing that a character could never be or have any reality unless the roots of his present being could be shown to come out of the past. "Take me," he said good humoredly, "unless you know some stories from my youth, you'd never know why I'm the way I am today. When I was about ten I was the ugliest redhead and didn't have a friend. One day I stole a gun from my brother Claude and sold it. With the money I invited all the kids I could find to come to the drugstore and have sodas on me. My popularity lasted until the money was gone and then I was alone again.

Then at Yale I was a gaunt, gauche, homely country boy and made to feel by all the others just that way. So for weeks I had no one to talk to and I didn't go anywhere."

Lewis appeared to be insecure about everything: his personal life, his stature as a writer, his position in American letters and history, his lack of social graces. He lived much of his life in misery because he couldn't settle for what he had, but continued to want he knew not what.

He personified the restlessness of America. He dreaded being tied to anything or anyone. Yet the restlessness he suffered largely stemmed from his lack of ties or bonds. He called loneliness, "the old devil himself" and when it descended over him he was accustomed to, "sit back, look the devil in the eye and get ready."

"You can't fight it, Ida," he once said, talking about the aloneness of human beings, "so just relax and it will pass."

For Lewis anticipation was one of the few things which ever gave him any satisfaction. He was a man who seldom enjoyed the present, only occasionally reflected on the past, but most eagerly lived in the future, hoping vainly that what he sought would, upon realization, not evaporate, but rather satisfy him as nothing ever had. Because of his driving nature, however, he did not allow himself the pleasure of suspense, and dissipated his only source of joy by immediate action.

When he returned from Europe in the summer of 1949 he was so excited about the gifts which were in his trunk for his household staff that he rushed immediately to the hall and the unopened trunk after the first greetings took place, in spite of guests Richard Llewellyn and myself who were waiting for dinner. He carelessly dumped his personal possessions on the floor until he located the presents, which he promptly distributed. This done, he was let down; the excitement was gone and his eyes said "so what?"

Lewis was a man who ran each race faster and harder than the preceding one; a person who won the trophy each time without stopping to reflect why he did it, and then in a flash found another race to enter. He gave the impression that if he stopped in between the sprints for too long he would cease to be. This endless chain of races was his only definition, his salvation and his death in one.

For the most part Lewis was extremely inept in his relationships with people. A sudden enthusiasm for a person could abruptly turn to dislike. A more sustained friendship often finished in boredom. Unless someone just happened to know, to understand, and was willing to make concessions, friendships invariably ended in a rubble heap. He rarely used the word "friend" and often said "It's one of the most misused words in the American vocabulary." He substituted phrases like "someone I know" or "someone who lived in the same town." He knew many people, was fond of them at a distance, but a steady diet of any one person resulted in a disappointment for both Lewis and the individual involved.

One of the very few who remained on close terms with him over many years was Carl Van Doren. Carl and I decided that for any person to survive in a friendship with Lewis he had to have a keen intuitive sense and a perception which operated spontaneously with every occasion that arose and every mood Lewis experienced.

Lewis had invited guests all through the summer months of 1947. He always looked forward to his friends' arrival, but began inquiring and planning for their departure almost as soon as the greetings took place. His compulsion to keep on the move drove him to push other people. Bennett Cerf, the head of Random House, which published Lewis' books, and his wife Phyllis stayed at Thorvale a few days that summer. Bennett and Phyllis were asked to enjoy the resort features of Lewis' estate, but it was a sprint from beginning to end. Lewis suggested that the Cerfs play tennis. A few preliminaries were necessary: getting on rubber sole shoes, finding the racquets and balls, and finally walking up to the court. They had just begun to warm up when Lewis appeared as a spectator, watched a few volleys, decided the Cerfs had had enough tennis for one day and pushed them along to the swimming pool for a nice cooling plunge before lunch. Lewis had Bennett and Phyllis in and out of the pool and rushing up to the house for lunch before they were even aware of what the water felt like. More of the same sort of program filled each day, with the Cerfs ending their visit in near exhaustion.

Lewis disliked inviting people to visit him formally because it meant issuing the invitation in advance. Although he never gave the reason for this peculiar behavior, it was apparent that a principal factor was his utter and complete distaste of being tied to an obligation. Further, he couldn't be sure that the person whom he invited on Monday for dinner on Friday, would be the person he would care to see or be with when Friday was at hand. Unfortunately, not even for him would a casual acquaintance be willing to drop everything and appear on ten minutes notice for a dinner engagement. And people must be acquaintances before becoming good friends. He had a habit of telling people to drop in to see him anytime. And when occasionally an unsuspecting soul took him at his word and just stopped by informally, he would grit his teeth, get through a small visit, then go into the house exhausted, cursing people's stupidity and ill manners.

Lewis loved to talk and he liked an audience, and his greatest pleasure came from being the leading man with a group serving as a good supporting cast over which he could shine. Participating in no athletics and indulging in chess as an only pastime, talking became a hobby and his principal form of relaxation.

He disliked anyone who agreed with him arbitrarily. If anyone chose to challenge his viewpoint, however, he would become irate and ill mannered, even when that person happened to be a guest in his home. But Lewis could very easily take an opposite stand on the same subject at a later time, particularly if the person to whom he was then talking had a leaning toward the other point of view.

It was difficult for him to believe that people could be happy with the routine life he saw them live or heard about in a small town like Williamstown or anywhere. He envied them and hated them at the same time. He called marriage, home, and family "that dreadful thing, a 'Solidly Established Life'"; but he missed it. Lewis was wistfully envious of what he didn't have; what he wanted, but could not enjoy.

Lewis seldom noticed what he ate at home and rarely commented on the food prepared by his cook. He did, however, love sweets at all times. Three brightly decorated cookie jars were always filled with hermits, brownies and his favorite chocolate chip cookies and kept on a lower shelf in the pantry at Thorvale. After an evening of chess or music and talk, he would leave the living room and wander into the kitchen, reappearing with as many cookies as his hands would hold, offering me one, then finishing the rest himself. Alma, who cooked for him the last year at Thorvale, delighted in making the "gooiest" desserts she could find in any cookbook. He rarely ate much of the main course at dinner, but never failed to finish the pie, cake or pastry. Influenced by the Italian custom of finishing a meal with fruit, cheese and crackers, Lewis had suggested to Alma that she occasionally substitute these things for the customary sweet. But after the first time, he remarked, "Hell, isn't there something sweet for dessert?" Alma wisely forgot to remember the continental custom thereafter.

During much of his writing career Lewis had many secretary-companions who helped him to obtain background material for his novels. He hired Barnaby Conrad to serve in this capacity in the Spring of 1947 when both of them were in California. Lewis was in Hollywood working on a motion picture script and consulting with a studio which was making a film of his novel, *Cass Timberlane*. Barnaby, only a few years out of Yale but already experienced as a bullfighter in Spain, was living with his parents in Santa Barbara. He had written to Lewis asking for a meeting, introducing himself as a budding writer. This meeting in turn led to Lewis' inviting Barnaby to come to Thorvale. It was another of Lewis' sudden plunges into a relationship which was to end abruptly, in about five months.

Barnaby was writing his first novel during those summer months and Lewis was extremely encouraging and helpful in giving him plenty of time to write. Barnaby was without a doubt in those early newlywed days of secretaryship Lewis' vision of God's gift to him. Barnaby had learned how to play chess, immediately and well, before coming to Williamstown. He could play the piano by ear and cleverly accompanied the dinner chimes much to Lewis' delight and amusement. He was a gifted artist and could sketch, draw or paint, with not too many artistic demands to fulfill his needs. He could remember names excellently and was brilliant as a companion and secretary on more formal occasions where guests were involved. He liked people, but he could also go it alone, if Lewis chose to cut himself off from guests. And Barnaby was writing with a certain dedication and persistence, which even Lewis could not help admire.

The summer of 1947 was a good one for Lewis despite many reasons for it to be otherwise. Marcella Powers, a young actress and literary agent with whom Lewis had had a liaison for over seven years, had left him and married a younger man during the previous spring. But enough things were happening in the newness of his surroundings to help relieve the shock and pain. There had been enough attention paid to *Kingsblood Royal* so that he had swallowed the adverse criticism without too much resentment. He wasn't drinking and he was working on the beginning of *The God-Seeker*.

He was surrounded by Joseph Hardrick, his cook and chauffeur, Alma and Wilson Perkins, who cleaned and took care of the estate, and Barnaby. Lewis was having his house redone to please his particular needs and the grounds were being cleaned and landscaped meticulously. He had frequent guests, including Max Flowers, formerly of the Williams College Theatre department, and his wife Jo, who were heading up the student group at the Berkshire Playhouse in Stockbridge nearby. He was invited to the homes of neighbors William H. Vanderbilt, a former governor of Rhode Island, O. Dixon Marshall, a local attorney and Cornelia Stratton Parker, an author originally from California.

His loneliness was less in evidence and his restlessness seemed momentarily to have slackened. He was in fairly good health and walked miles exploring his hundreds of acres, with no little pretense at being the country squire in old New England. It was as if he had imagined this role in the past, picturing himself as content in just such surroundings, and concluding that he was typecast for this way of life. With something of the same kind of determination that an actor must have when first rehearsing for a play, getting the feel of the plot and the interplay with other characters, Lewis had thrown himself into the role of gentleman farmer/writer with a kind of naive hopefulness that this, at last, would be the life for him.

Of all the guests at Thorvale, Carl Van Doren was the only one who maintained an easy, relaxed relationship with Lewis regardless of the length of time he stayed. Carl, whom Barnaby described as being "anyone's father", merely overlooked Lewis' bustling manner and in his calm way went quietly about in his own fashion which, in turn, had the same effect on Lewis. Lewis came to accept Carl's goings and comings as if he were a regular part of the household and his compulsion to "order things" for Carl vanished.

During one of his many pleasant visits, he and Lewis walked down to the swimming pool, located beside a brook in a charming, woodsy area away from the house. They found me swimming there.

"Hi", was Lewis' usual greeting; he sort of chirped it. "How's the water?" Before I had a chance to answer he asked "Where's Barny?" I pointed over to the brook where Barnaby was fishing. Carl said "Come on out and talk with us." They had drawn back into the shade, sitting on beach chairs. This was one of the rare times when Lewis was peaceful and relaxed.

"We took a walk up through that path," said Lewis, waving his hand over to the left, "If you'd stop playing golf or swimming, you ought to follow it someday."

"Wait 'til she gets old, Red," Carl laughingly suggested. "Walking is about all *we* can do!

Lewis was wonderfully amusing when he was at ease. That evening he was especially so. He had invited Alfred Hooper, the English mathematician, for dinner. Hooper was living in the very small town of Pownal, Vermont just north of Williamstown. We discussed new books, country living and the Tanglewood concerts which were about to begin. Lewis had been invited to attend as a guest of William Vanderbilt, who had a box for the occasion. He had accepted, but the idea of a box annoyed him. Music was music and he could see no reason for all the "do" that had been whipped up in recent years for this festival. It was a country affair, tickets should be one price, and he thought the fanfare was completely ridiculous.

Later the discussion got around to interior decorating. Lewis held forth on the latest trends in homemaking. The American home of moneyed people, he said, no more reflected their taste or personality than if they camped out in a lean-to. Carl suggested that there might be "little things" after an interior decorator finished that marked the house as a home. "Hell, no, Carl! It used to be that you could tell by the books you found lying around. But now the color consultant determines what goes on the damn book shelves; the homeowners order a set of something in red or green leather. Why there's no need for anything to be between the covers; nobody would know the difference!"

It was dusk when we finally left the table and headed toward the front veranda, looking toward Mount Greylock. The music of a recording of Berlioz' "Harold in Italy" came out to us through the open doors, darkness came on, and the beacon on Mount Greylock twinkled in the distance. The woods and fields came alive with night noises, and the group lapsed into a comfortable silence which continued after the music stopped.

"You know", Lewis said, "if I had advice to give to a young man today about marriage and the kind of girl he should marry, I know what I'd say." His voice brought everyone's thoughts back to the fold. Carl ventured that he wouldn't dare give any advice but Lewis went on, "Well, Carl, I'd tell him not to think about her looks, how much money she had, or how affectionate she was, but ask whether he could live with this woman's conversation for the rest of his life." And then after a long pause I said "I think, Red, I'd add whether he could also live with her silences."

The group then turned to various opinions about what type of woman would make a perfect wife and whether there was such an animal. Lewis then improvised a story of such a wife, the woman who did no wrong, who anticipated her husband's every need and desire, neither demanding nor complaining, never moody or ailing, pretty to look at and physically attractive, a good wife and excellent mother, perceptive of her husband's temperament, sensitive to his unspoken thoughts. Lewis sketched the slow, tortuous path of frustration for the husband when he finds no cause for disagreement, no momentary burst of anger, no possibility for a fight where he might emerge the victor. The climax comes when he can bear it no longer, contemplates murdering his wife, planning to waylay her in the kitchen with a hammer. But she enters the room by another door, comes up behind him and smilingly tells him to put the hammer away and go upstairs for a nap because he needs rest.

"And that," said Lewis, "is what men think they want but would be crazy with." The story unrolled with the fluidity of an oft repeated tale, completely filled in with descriptions of both wife and husband and the acidity of Lewis' incisive scorn.

Lewis' incredible facility in devising plots on the spur of the moment made it easy to believe that at age 25 he had begun to sell story outlines to such authors as Jack London and Albert Payson Terhune.

Lewis, who had been married and divorced twice, continued after a pause "Men have got to marry something, but isn't it a pity it's a woman. Women and war have a lot in common; men fight both of them and seldom bother to question why."

Carl, whose marital experiences had not been completely blissful, answered, "Sorry, Red, I don't agree with you; women are still the most civilized influence we have, in spite of the problems they present."

"Well, you may be right, Carl, but maybe what I mean is that we Americans have ruined women for the "Virgin role" Henry Adams talks about in his *Education*. It's that chapter on the "Virgin" and the "Dynamo". He talks about the "Virgin Image" being the highest energy source ever known to man. And he compares the ineffectiveness of our dynamos in America with the influence of the "Virgin" and "Venus" in Europe throughout the ages. Carl, we just don't have an "American Virgin" who commands, and I agree with Adams that an "American Virgin" would never dare exist. Our American women, even though they have been emancipated, are no positive force in this country."

Carl agreed with the Henry Adams thesis but quietly brought the discussion to an end by suggesting, "Red, have you considered that the American woman is probably what American man wants her to be? If her force in this country has become mechanical rather than feminine, who but man is to blame?

It's values, Red."

Lewis' relationships with people were replete with sudden, bewildering reversals. It was never a slow process outwardly. The change of mind smoldered within him, with no external evidence for some time. When he finally announced the change it could be unbelievably abrupt.

His Thorvale estate included a farmhouse. When he bought it it was occupied by the Bishop family, who had been there for years as tenant farmers. Lewis liked them when he first bought the estate, so he kept up the arrangement. He was overly generous, kind and glowing with praise to me about their work, their products and management, laughingly adding that it was fortunate he was not dependent on "the cows and their whims; the chickens and their temperament for an income."

He did let the Bishops know about the expense of new farm machinery which he bought on their advice, and the remodeling of parts of the farm house for a returning veteran son and wife; but he voiced no words of criticism. Instead of questioning them on each new demand or gently reminding them of the deficit they were causing, he let the whole situation ride. Then without warning he suddenly turned like an infuriated animal, deciding to release them immediately, dispose of the farm and bring the whole arrangement to a halt. The farmers never had a hint of his dissatisfaction. He abruptly told them they were through and gave them only one month to move. Kindness turned to stony obstinacy; generosity became ruthlessness and the guardian angel became the devil. The consequences were tragic for the family, but he seemed completely untouched by their plight. The farmer and his wife were well over fifty, had done nothing but farm all their lives, had saved up little if any money and had no place to go. They asked for more time; they pleaded for another chance, but Lewis showed no leniency. His insistence on the time limit was completely unnecessary and cruel. He had no immediate plans for the farm house. His agent had no prospects for a sale. Nevertheless he stuck to his original ultimatum with the same drive to "finish" the affair as he used in his work and other aspects of living. He did it, also, because he wanted the people whose lives he had affected to be out of sight so that their presence would not bother his conscience.

But the human element tormented him. For months afterwards he would bring up the subject and attempt to show that he had not been unfair in his decision. With the same technique he used in writing novels, he became so obsessed with the facts as he embroidered them that he would be momentarily convinced he was completely right and the evicted farmers all wrong.

Lewis vacillated in his religious beliefs over the years probing, challenging and finally remaining adamant in his complete disbelief in a Superior Being. I asked him about his interest in Protestantism and he defensively answered, "There are two menaces today — catholicism and communism — they have much in common, and they definitely are threats to progress."

On one occasion Lewis accepted an invitation to speak at a men's dinner at the Williamstown First Congregational Church. George Bielby, the church's minister, later reported that Lewis discussed the necessity of the Protestant church to find a way between religious authoritarianism and secular fascism. But he deplored the many divisions of Protestantism which handicapped its effectiveness. He further thought that a men's club could be a very useful instrument in promoting understanding between denominations.

After his talk George Bielby sounded out those present on the desirability of forming such a group. When enthusiasm for such a move became evident the group proceeded to receive nominations from the floor for the office of president of the new men's club. Two or three names were proposed. At this point Lewis turned to George and said, "May I say another word, George?" He jumped to his feet and spoke with great irritation,

"I remember a meeting which occurred a long time ago in an upper room. The effect of that meeting has been great. But, gentlemen, they didn't sit around electing a President, Vice-President, Secretary and Treasurer of the organization. If there is anything that can hamstring an active group it is to appoint officers and committee members in great numbers. If you are going to have a men's club why don't you just come together without all the fuss of organization? Now I take my leave and you can talk about me all you want." With that he strode out, and that was the last he was ever seen around the confines of the First Congregational Church.

III

During our very first evening together at Thorvale Farm I sensed that Lewis was bearing a grudge against Williams College and wanted assurance that his adverse opinion of the college, the faculty and the student body was justified. Eventually I pieced together what lay behind this. The clues came in bits; from Lewis when he was off guard, from Carl Van Doren who knew Lewis' ambition, and from Barnaby, who supplied factual details.

Lewis had expected to be socially overwhelmed by the President of Williams and invited immediately to be a guest lecturer at the college. He had also hoped that the most important members of the English department would seek him out and eagerly carry him high on their shoulders into their classrooms as a famous American author, winner of the Nobel Prize and founder of a new kind of American novel. He had gambled on what he thought was a sure thing: a writer in the cordial atmosphere of the intellectual community of a small college noted for its social life and interest in scholarly pursuits. Certainly he would be welcomed and accepted, even urged to become a part of the life of the college. But, alas, this did not happen.

Lewis asked Luther Mansfield of the Williams English department to give him a small party to meet some of Luther's friends. He had met Luther when Luther was at Swarthmore. At the party Lewis was at his charming best. Many invitations came in the weeks which followed, but he kept offering excuses for not accepting. Short of the President of the College or the Head of the English department, any other faculty member's attempts to welcome him were only bitter reminders of what he had expected. The disappointment bloomed into bitterness.

Part of the problem was Lewis' own fault; part was due to a certain protective aloofness among members of the Williams community. Lewis could not see that pride and awe would prevent people from seeking him out and overwhelming him with the warm welcome he had anticipated. His genuinely humble feeling about himself made him totally unfamiliar with the average man's reactions to someone "great". He didn't meet reserved reactions in the Middle West where he was born and grew up. The "boys" just openly greeted their former neighbor and invited him on a fishing trip or a family picnic. Unfortunately at the various times he chose to settle in the East his repeated experiences taught him nothing. He had tried Connecticut and then told bitter tales of the "snobbishness" of the inhabitants. He had tried Vermont only to come to the same conclusion.

Lewis' choice of Williamstown was based on the premise that college people are more intellectual, and less apt to be provincial in their social ideas and inhibitions. He longed desperately for a group without social barriers and petty formalities, a group that would accept him as he was, never realizing that such a Utopia would never exist for a person like himself.

As I came to know Lewis it became clear that he very much wanted recognition, but not the kind of the best selling author on the top of a list. The movie-idol type of idolatry annoyed him to the point of insolence. The autograph hunter, the "Oh, there's Sinclair Lewis" enthusiasts were easy marks for his sarcasm and irony. What he sought was the kind of praise and honor granted to the people who had reached the highest echelons in such areas as science or medicine; an esteem which endured and carried a kind of dignified prestige. He wanted to be recognized as someone who had contributed something to a cause, not just as someone whose recognition was based on the rate of speed at which another sure-fire novel appeared on the bookshelves.

"Americans don't know when a man has devoted his life to them." he would say, or, "We're bourgeois compared to Europeans who recognize the place of authors in society"; and "A stupid business tycoon rates more esteem than creative writers in America."

The tension with the college became heightened by a rather unfortunate incident involving one of the few faculty members with whom he had become friendly. The director of the Williams College Theatre, Max Flowers, and his wife, Jo, had endeared themselves to Lewis in many ways. Max was from the Midwest which made him almost a blood relative. Jo was a wonderful New Englander: honest, outspoken and socially at ease, with the magnificent knack of making one feel like an old friend within moments after an introduction. Unfortunately, just as their friendship was developing the college administration dropped Max for reasons which were never clarified, and which could be taken as being due in large part to faculty politics.

Lewis was extremely helpful to the Flowers. He offered them without charge a cottage on his estate while Max looked for an appointment elsewhere. He introduced Max to friends in the professional theatre. When he was unable to find suitable work in either the academic or professional theatre Lewis obtained through friends in Minneapolis jobs for both Max and Jo in retail stores there. This was one of the many demonstrations of how intensely loyal and helpful a friend Lewis could be, while the friendship lasted.

The dismissal of Max Flowers gave Lewis a reason outside of himself to dislike the college. His bitterness and rancor tripled in intensity. He howled at the unfairness of the incident. He soliloquized brilliantly on the administration, the faculty and student body in the same biting, satiric fashion which he had used in *Babbitt* and *Elmer Gantry.*

"They're all little men on the faculty from what I've seen of them," Lewis snarled. "Have you met anyone you think is good?"

I had just finished one of the finest courses I had ever taken under Frederick Schuman in the Political Science Department, and I felt that Schuman had one of the keenest, sharpest minds I had ever encountered. And, although I wasn't quite certain what Lewis meant by "little men," I hadn't felt that any of the faculty I had met at Williams were little in any sense of the word.

"I wonder if you're not just hero worshiping" he said to me. "I've met Schuman and know some of the stuff he writes, but why is he content to stay in this goddam smug community if he's any good?"

One of the most unfortunate episodes with the college happened in the fall of 1947. Lewis had left Thorvale in early September on a trip through Minnesota to gather material for his novel *The God-Seeker*. It included visits to the University of Minnesota and various friends in and around Minneapolis. Besides gathering information, Lewis was looking for another secretary-companion for the winter months to replace Barnaby who had left in August; someone who might also help him with research for the new book. On his return Lewis announced that he had found a young man, James Roers, to serve his needs. He was a graduate student at the University of Minnesota but was willing to postpone his studies. Lewis eagerly pointed out that I could introduce him socially and see to it that he met young people. Jim was not to arrive until about a week later, but plans were made immediately for a welcoming dinner at which Jo Flowers and I were to take him under our wings and make him feel at home. The night of the dinner I first joined Jo for a cocktail first at her place on the estate. She had already met Jim and found him to be a shy, insecure young man, probably a very good student, but lacking in the sophistication which living with Lewis required. She wondered how long he would last.

We joined Lewis and Jim in the living room before dinner. Jim had little opportunity to say anything because Lewis was nervously going over his plans for him while he was at Thorvale. It sounded as if he wanted to be certain that every spare moment Jim had would be fully occupied. I had become experienced at sensing when Lewis regretted doing something which had committed him in a way not easily avoided. It had only taken him from noon that day to realize that his invitation to Jim had been a mistake. He talked too eagerly and boastfully about how he had concluded that Jim was exactly the right man for him.

Jim was a pleasant but unpolished young man, understandably ill at ease. One was aware of him at the dinner table in the kind of way one is aware of a young offspring just experimenting with joining his elders at dinner. A tension developed. Conversation, which ordinarily flowed easily around the table, went in little jerks and starts. Lewis, unguardedly, would stop to watch and observe. I knew then that something would break to see to it that Jim Roers left.

Lewis interrupted one of the long silences with the suggestion that Jim get started immediately on the book research at the Williams College Library. "Ida, tomorrow Jim can drive to town with Jo, and you can introduce him to Mr. Wright (the College Librarian). He can get started right away and round up some of the information I need."

The idea was wrong to begin with. If Lewis wanted Jim to use the library he certainly should have been the person to introduce him and get the necessary permission. But, hesitating for only a moment, I agreed to call Bill Wright in the morning. Lewis continued the conversation with stories about Williamstown winters and the kind of solitude Jim might expect in this part of the country. Jim reacted like an unmanned boat; he rose with the swells and subsided in the troughs. Yet he had a reassuring unemotional kind of stability. I didn't feel he would capsize.

Bill Wright, the Librarian, happened to be out of town. Knowing that Lewis would not want the secretary to waste time, I introduced him to the reference librarian, who suggested, however, that Jim wait for Mr. Wright's return before working in the stacks.

When Lewis checked with Jim that evening about his day's work and learned that he had not been allowed into the stacks, the Lewis rage shook Thorvale. Although it was a late hour he called a couple of members of the English department and shouted about the day's incident and warned them that all the New York papers would carry an article about how Williams College had treated him. "Never have I heard of a college forbidding the use of its stacks by an American author or any other author!" He listened to no explanations and would accept no apologies.

Lewis sent Jim to New York the very next morning ostensibly to work in the public library there. Although Lewis kept him on salary for several months he never sent him any work to do. He closed himself in to write *The God-Seeker* without help from anyone.

IV

Sinclair Lewis made something of a fetish out of a daily routine living pattern. He kept lists of "things to do" like a good housewife's shopping reminder. And he admitted he often included such trivia as "wash teeth" in order to have the satisfaction of crossing off an item as accomplished.

He was extremely thrifty in little ways. He would tie a broken rubber band together and keep it for further use. He always kept a supply of old, used envelopes on the backs of which he scribbled notes; he boasted of wearing a twenty year old tweed jacket. He insisted on having an old fountain pen repaired instead of buying a new one. His chauffeur drove an old touring car, gleaming like new, which dated back to the 1930's.

It was a penny wise, pound foolish frugality, since the maintenance of these old possessions was often far more expensive than new replacements. I think he enjoyed the illusion of being economical. These spurious thrift practices were probably derived from his early childhood and later adolescent experiences with a frugal father who carefully doled out money and constantly reminded his son of the evil of overspending.

His miserly little ways were also a means of compensating for extravagant expenditures. He never questioned the cook who purchased food for the household at outlandish prices. He kept three or four people in his employ constantly. The upkeep of his huge estate was exorbitantly high. He traveled everywhere in this country and abroad luxuriously. And when he thought he would like his own fresh eggs (this after he sold the farm on his property) he had a magnificent chicken house built, with the finest heating system money could buy, and with a view of Mount Greylock which would have thrilled the most indifferent human being, not to mention chickens. He jokingly alluded to the chicken house as Lewis' folly and reflected that if he were fortunate enough to live to the age of 100 and the chickens laid eggs at prodigious rates, each egg would cost him only about ten dollars.

He was fastidious about his surroundings, particularly his study where he did his writing. Occasionally in a reminiscent mood he would laugh at the way he had done his early writing — "standing in the kitchen, using the top of an old fashioned wash tub, or cramped in a chair, using anything available to scribble on." But this was from necessity when money was lacking. His workroom at Thorvale was a writer's paradise, designed to his detailed specifications, including a three-way desk, with a roll chair to slide from typewriter to open reference books or to other source material, carefully spread out and arranged for immediate use. The four walls were lined from floor to ceiling with reference books, many of them rare collector's items, and in one section he had copies of his own books. On the binding of each one was a white notebook ring reinforcement, indicating that this was a "work copy" of the title. When he wasn't writing the study was immaculate, more like an ascetic's retreat; not a pencil, index card or scrap of paper exposed. He was as highly organized in his writing as a first rate executive.

In spite of many episodes of drinking excessively over the years, he still persisted, inebriated or sober, in keeping to a rigid schedule for work, exactly as if he were punching a factory time clock. In many ways he was as conservative as the characters he created and riddled with scorn. I think it could be shown that his revolts against conformity in his life stemmed from forced bravado. They were attempts to break with early puritanical training and family traditions which were a basic part of him and from which he never successfully freed himself. Self discipline came naturally to him and therefore he was completely intolerant of aspiring young writers who bemoaned the hurdle of making themselves work.

The summer when Barnaby Conrad was Lewis' secretary, Lewis felt a great warmth for this budding author, until he realized that Barnaby was not a worker as he, Lewis, always had been. When one night Barnaby complained of not feeling like writing the agreed upon number of words per day, Lewis flew off into a fury. "Barny! When will you learn that you write whether you feel like it or not? You'll never do anything if you wait until the mood moves you."

Barnaby protested mildly, "But what's the use of writing two chapters if I know that they're not what I want to say and they don't come up to the writing I've done before?"

This was enough for Lewis to go off in his high pitched voice, showing intense annoyance that someone could even aspire to be a writer and not follow the kind of routine he had imposed on himself all of his life. "No muse ever moved me. If I had waited for inspiration I would never have written even one book. You young writers don't know what it is to work. You all feel that there's something privileged about your ability. Just because you write one story and get it published, you think that you can sit back and wait for something else to happen. Well, it doesn't. You work for it and you sweat. You write words and pages and then you do them over again."

When Lewis began a soliloquy of this kind no one even thought of interrupting. Eventually of its own momentum it became a sort of sermon. As the excitement of his own words gave birth to more and more ideas he often ended up sounding like one of his own character creations.

But there was no doubt that Lewis was a dedicated man. Part

of the dedication came from his doctor father, who had devoted his life to caring for the small community at Sauk Centre; and something in that early background made him feel that a man must serve his fellowman in some way. Writing as an art form, to be indulged in by the few who appreciated it, was not his idea of a man's purpose in life. Never did I hear him speak of writing in pretentiously artistic terms. There was something down to earth in his attitude toward writing, just as there is in a Minnesota farmer's feeling about the butter he produces or the corn he grows.

Most authors have their own special ways of "letting down steam" after completing a major work. Carl Van Doren told of going to six movies, one right after another, after finishing the manuscript for *The Autobiography of Ben Franklin*. This was his way of relieving the shock of completion and insuring that the overtones of a finished job would not be unbearable. Lewis laughed at Carl's explanation of this need. "When I'm finished with something, I'm finished. I'm just restless to get started on something else." In effect he was saying that he did not know how to relax. Work drove him and he drove himself to work. Nowhere was there room to enjoy the success of a finished job, the feeling of satisfaction that comes from creation regardless of the reception of a book. Shortly after the publication of *Kingsblood Royal* in the early summer of 1947, Lewis went vigorously to work on a play, untitled and never published or produced. But it had demanded a scheduled routine of writing every day all summer. It was as if without writing he had no reason for being.

In writing to me from Florence in the winter of 1949 he said "It's an enchanted colony in an enchanted town, and the king of it all is B.B. (Bernard Berenson), the greatest authority on Italian cinquecento art — but I doubt if I'd ever work here, and so much of the horrid New England puritanism I do have. I feel guilty without work."

One evening he gave his own account of the intensity with which he wrote. "A man with a regular job doesn't know how lucky he is. He works so many hours a day, gets paid for the work, and when he is done the rest of the time is his. A writer owes his life, or feels he does, to the public. He's never through saying what he has to say. Then there's always the research you have to do before you write a book. It would appear to someone outside that a trip such as I took through the South for *Kingsblood* was a pleasure, but it wasn't. It was demanding. You train yourself to observe and be alert for details and situations. It's like being an actor for every minute of the day and then writing down your lines for future use. That trip was work, more work than sitting at the typewriter afterwards and writing the damn book. Do you know that every book I ever wrote was done from accurate notes I had worked on for months, sometimes years in advance?"

Later I saw the scholarly, methodical way in which each of Lewis' books came into being, including his little notebook with a list of names and after each a notation of whether it had been used before and in which book or story he had used it. This was to avoid repetition. He gave me a work copy of *Cass Timberlane,* in the front of which is a list of pages indicating places in the book where he wrote in a way he did not like and did not want to repeat in other books.

"I haven't had a real vacation since I started writing", Lewis said, "but a man with a job has so many weeks vacation every year, and weekends are all his." Whether literally he had not had the "vacation" he spoke of, Lewis didn't take time off while I knew him. His writing and his life were one. Without the writing Lewis ceased to be. It was his definition of being. Consequently he drove himself to continue, even when he knew, but would not admit, that he no longer was writing what he wanted to write.

"Another thing, even when I'm on vacation physically, I'm

always at work mentally." At times he would dwell for sometime on this topic. One time I allowed that I couldn't understand why the satisfaction of a completed book wouldn't be enough release to produce a relaxed period in his life. I got no direct response but, as was his habit, he took off on a sort of tangential line and said "Chess is better than movies, I think. It's one kind of thinking instead of another. Let's play a game now."

Lewis' mind could not vacation. He was always thinking; and thinking about his work was easier than thinking about life, which was painful. His mind was on duty every waking minute, gathering, fashioning relationships and devising interpretations. This kind of absorption doesn't allow for much wholehearted exchange of views and feelings with others. Most of the give and take of human relationships was something he missed all along the way. And without it he suffered an inner loneliness, the kind he describes in *Dodsworth,* in *Main Street* and in *Babbitt.*

Lewis' books are not complicated. Lewis was never obscure in his writing, not by design and not even spontaneously. He thought clearly and worked systematically. He loved to tell stories, and they were obvious in plot and in characterization and purpose. Few, if any, have any symbolism. There's little complex psychological motivation of his characters. He was not poetically inspired in the sense of a Dylan Thomas, nor philosophically involved as was Albert Camus. He was an expert craftsman and he worked methodically at writing as would a good carpenter or plumber at his trade. He was volcanic in the sense that he had so much to say, but he was disciplined and never erupted chaotically.

Lewis had none of the pretentious approach to writing nor the commonly accepted version of the artist's way of life. He knew little about art, music or the dance. He owned hundreds of recordings of which he recognized only a very few. He owned four original Childe Hassam paintings, but seemed to have no particular reason for having them. He had visited endless art galleries and famous cathedrals in Europe, but almost as a sense of duty and as a means to an end. It added to the knowledge he might someday want.

Lewis had the daring and vitality to write about subjects with a critical force, thereby chancing society's condemnation. He turned his devastating analysis to small towns in *Main Street*, to businessmen in *Babbitt*, to scientists in *Arrowsmith*, to wives in *Dodsworth*, to preachers in *Elmer Gantry*. Since his writing was so acid, so penetrating in its probing and criticism, why, one would ask, wasn't it rejected? Why was he so widely read?

In *Babbitt* he was ruthless in ridiculing Babbitt's lack of individuality. He was razor sharp in underscoring Babbitt's spiritual shallowness; still at the same time Lewis gave Babbitt a touch of refreshing and attractive naivete and innocent youthfulness. It was this combination of truthful laceration softened by a comforting poultice which led the American public to accept his writing.

Lewis' criticisms were softened by a basic affection for the very thing he felt compelled to ridicule. In a sense he was criticizing himself, too. He smote sentimentality successfully, because at heart, he was a sentimentalist and a romanticist. He mocked the cruder manifestations of Yankee Imperialism, but, he too, was a fanatic American. He could laugh at himself heartily and he transferred that laugh to America. He dipped his pen in acid to etch on the minds of his readers the situation as it was, showing them what it could and ought to be.

Carl Van Doren said of him "Not one of Lewis' contemporaries has kept so close to the main channel of American life as he or so near to the human surface. He is part channel and part surface. To venture into hyperbole, not only is he an American telling stories, but he is America telling stories."

In his essay *Self Portrait*, Lewis observes, "Whether or not there is any merit in my books, I do not know and I do not vastly care, since I have had the somewhat exhausting excitement of writing them. But, good or not, they have in them everything I have been able to get from life or give to life; there is really no Sinclair Lewis about whom even that diligent scribbler himself could write, outside of what appears in his characters. All his respect for learning, for integrity, for accuracy and for the possibilities for human achievement is to be found not in the rather hectic, exaggerative man as his intimates saw him, but in his portrait of Professor Max Gottlieb in *Arrowsmith*. Most of the fellow's capacity for loyalty to love and friendship has gone into Leora in the same novel, and into the account of George F. Babbitt's affection for his son. And whatever potentialities for hard, lean Lindbergh courage this Lewis, this product of the pioneer forests and wheat fields of Minnesota, may once have had, has seemingly all gone into the depiction of such characters as Will Kennicott, the resolute country doctor in *Main Street*."

Most every actor before he becomes a star has an idol; most every painter aspires to another who has preceded him; most every writer has another writer before him as a model. Lewis' paragon was Charles Dickens. But on this matter as on others, Lewis was like a sensitive child who wants something but doesn't come out and ask for it directly. He hinted at it, talked around it, but hesitated to be explicit.

Prominent on his bookshelf in the living room at Thorvale was the beautiful Nonesuch Press edition of Dickens. Lewis often commented on the beautiful colors of the bindings and with pretended ridicule added that the books were in the living room because the colors blended with the decor. He would casually remark about the similarity of his choice of names for his characters and those Dickens used. He seldom missed an opportunity to mention the important role Dickens played in English letters and the high regard the English people had for him as a writer. He spoke of the brilliance of Dickens' style and the fact that he could read and re-read any of Dickens' books and always find something new and surprising. He once said jokingly, "Dickens and the Bible will never go out of print." And on another occasion, "When they have removed all authors from required reading in schools and substituted visual education, little boys and girls and young men and women will seek out Dickens, even if it is considered to be subversive literature, and he will be the saviour of mankind."

I had hoped that sometime he would discuss what he thought about the relationship of his own writing to that of Dickens'; and eventually he did. It was after Norman Mailler's visit and we were discussing new authors and the value of their books. Lewis wanted to know how I felt about *The Naked and The Dead,* and the place it might finally have in American literature. This led to the question of what makes an author live not only for his own age but for future generations. We had talked about this many evenings, but there was always something new to say.

"If my books are read fifty years from now," Lewis said, "it's because I did for America what Dickens did for England."

"Was this what you had in mind when you started writing?" I asked.

"In my first stuff I only wanted to write; I just wanted to tell stories, but I hoped that I would be able to create characters who would live, American types. I didn't do it until *Main Street* and in that the setting was perhaps as much the Dickens touch as Doc Kennicott or Carol. *Main Street* then was America. I had to write that story before I could say anything further. The man who lived on the Main Streets in America came next in *Babbitt.* It's like the theatre, you build the set and then you put your characters in it. It would have been too much to put Babbitt in *Main Street.*" And then after a pause he added "The titles of my books are straight Dickens." And like Dickens he created characters which have become part of a national culture.

The Nobel Prize was awarded to Lewis, for, among other reasons, "his vigorous and graphic art of description and his ability to create, with wit and humor, new types of people." To this the editors of *Nobel, the Man and His Prizes* added, "Lewis in *Babbitt* has created a figure the significance of which as a type has not been surpassed in contemporary literature, and in which his nation has recognized, with more or less satisfaction, its own image."

One of the major tragedies of Lewis' life was that he continued to write when it was no longer a spontaneous, explosive urge to say something. His last two books, in particular, were mostly the products of his compulsion to work, without the inspiration and creative force which marked his best work.

His last book was originally written under the title of *Over the Body of Lucy Jade,* and was concerned with the relationships between an American girl and expatriate Americans in Italy. It was extremely sad to have it turn out poorly. He failed to make the characters convincing, and it was replete with unfortunate anachronisms, having his 1950's characters, for example, speak in the cliches of the 1920's.

Bennett Cerf, Lewis' publisher, read the manuscript at Thorvale shortly after Lewis finished it in the summer of 1949. Bennett found it to be almost unpublishable. He telephoned me for help.

"Ida, I wonder if you could come out this afternoon and read it. Then perhaps if you and I can get Red into a conversation about it, it will be easier for me to tell him what I think."

When I arrived it was immediately obvious that great tension permeated the house. Moreover, Lewis wasn't very enthusiastic about my reading the manuscript. But despite the stresses of the situation I managed to finish it by early evening, after we had dinner. When in the discussion which followed Bennett attempted to slide gently into some of his criticisms, Lewis quickly went into one of his ferocious rages. It was a nightmare: bitter, loud, personal, and also sad and pathetic. He stormed at Bennett and threatened to change publishers. It went on for a long time, but eventually he became exhausted and went off to bed.

The next morning he was a little more conciliatory. But for days after Bennett left, Lewis threw abusive insult after insult at him, Random House and the world. He sank deeper and deeper into despair. But Bennett had done him a great service by refusing to publish it as it was. It would have been an embarrassment.

He eventually rewrote the book in Italy. In one of his letters from there in the following spring he wrote "I shall be busy with my book (which is so vast a change in and an improvement of *Lucy Jade* that you will not recognize it. Even a different title)." It was published after his death as *World So Wide*. He went back to *Dodsworth* for some of his characters, returning to what had once made him famous. It became, probably without intention, a brilliant staging for his exit.

Lewis had been drinking heavily when he was in Europe during the winter of 1948-1949. His general health gradually worsened even after he returned to Williamstown. In early spring he was overcome by a severe attack of pneumonia. I let his physician brother, Claude, know and in his understanding way he willingly came from Minnesota to help. By the middle of May Lewis had reasonably recovered. But after the *Lucy Jade* fiasco that summer he descended once again into a steady round of wine, gin and whiskey, which was to mark the beginning of the last phase of his life.

Often, when in his drunken stupor he raged uncontrollably about his friends, literary figures and his own importance. His attacks of sleepwalking were particularly frightening. Wilson Perkins, his houseman, would find him walking out of his room hugging a pillow, heading for the deadly staircase leading downstairs. Lewis' Williamstown physician, Dr. David Curtis, who had been compassionately and conscientiously trying to help, attempted to have him admitted to the local hospital. But they would not accept him as a patient in his delirious, alcoholic state. In desperation I telephoned Lewis' long standing doctor friend in New York, Dr. Cornelius Traeger. He got in touch with Dave Curtis and arranged for a schedule of medication and intravenous feeding. It was a dreadful and uncertain time. But after ten days or so, with the patience and close attention of Dave Curtis, he had passed through the worst of it. Although shaken and weak, he gradually resumed his walks and writing schedule. His thoughts turned to selling Thorvale and returning to Europe for good.

One day while dwelling on this subject as we walked along he turned to me and said "Darling, you have added enormously to my life during these past few years." And then after a pause, "How about going to Europe with me as Mrs. Sinclair Lewis?"

His manner was casual and tentative. But I felt myself almost trembling with bewilderment. As our friendship developed Lewis had long since won my strong admiration for what he had accomplished and for what he still was, despite all the complexities. But marriage? I thought of the great differences in our outlooks and our ages and Lewis' persistent record of impulsiveness and unpredictability. And I thought of my other interests. Moreover, strong doubts pressed in about whether I would be up to handling what probably lay ahead.

When Lewis confided in Bennett Cerf that he wished I would marry him, Bennett, with his ever present humor quipped to me in private "God, Ida, I can think of hundreds of beautiful chicks in New York alone who would grab the chance and scream "aye" without having ever seen the man." And, not intending to be cruel, but just Bennett, he added "You know it won't be for long, the way he's going. And you have so much to give each other." And then later, "Don't think of yourself, don't be that selfish, think of Red. You just might help to save the life of a great man."

In the end, however, my conservatism prevailed. And the

immediate situation was eased when his brother Claude consented to go to Europe with Lewis. As a physician he could be especially important. But I continued to be haunted about the correctness of my decision.

Early in September Lewis and his brother left for Europe on what was to be Lewis' last sail across the Atlantic. Depressed, with a hatred of Williamstown, he remarked, "I've given my life to this country in the best way, and no one cares."

Condensed Outline Biography of Sinclair Lewis

1885 Born in Sauk Centre, Minnesota, a town of less than 3000 about 100 miles northwest of Minneapolis, the last of three sons of his physician father
1908 Graduated from Yale University (officially a member of the Class of 1907)
1912 *Hike and the Aeroplane* published*
1914 Married Grace Hegger, on the staff of Vogue Magazine
Our Mr. Wrenn published
1915 *The Trail of the Hawk* published
1917 Son, Wells, born
The Job published
The Innocents published
1919 *Free Air* published
1920 *Main Street* published. International recognition
1922 *Babbitt* published
1924 *Arrowsmith* published
1925 Separated from Grace Hegger
1925 *Mantrap* published.
Awarded Pulitzer Prize for *Arrowsmith*; refused by Lewis
1927 *Elmer Gantry* published
1928 Marriage to Grace Hegger dissolved
Married Dorothy Thompson, well-known newspaper foreign correspondent
The Man Who Knew Coolidge published
1929 *Dodsworth* published
1930 Awarded Nobel Prize for Literature. First American author so honored.
Son, Michael, born
1932 *Ann Vickers* published

*The publication of Lewis' numerous short stories is not included in this outline.

1934 *Work of Art* published
1935 *It Can't Happen Here* published
1937 Separated from Dorothy Thompson
1938 *Prodigal Parents* published
1940 *Bethel Merriday* published
1942 Marriage to Dorothy Thompson dissolved
1943 *Gideon Planish* published
1944 Son, Wells, killed in action in France
1945 *Cass Timberlane* published
1947 *Kingsblood Royal* published
1949 *The God-Seeker* published
1951 Died in Rome at age 66
World So Wide published

About the Author

Sinclair Lewis first met Ida Compton as a result of her reviews of *Kingsblood Royal* in local Massachusetts newspapers, and they became close friends during his Williamstown years until he died in 1951. She was born in Pittsfield, Massachusetts in 1917, and died in 1985. She received an A.B. from Brenau College, and later was a graduate student at Williams College. In 1953 she married Charles Compton, a member of the Faculty. She had a great interest in literature, was broadly talented in business management and athletics, and had an extensive career in publishing, principally at the University of Chicago Press and Time, Inc.

About the Author

Sinclair Lewis first met Ida Compton as a result of her reviews of Kingsblood Royal in local Massachusetts newspapers, and they became close friends during his Williamstown years until he died in 1951. She was born in Pittsfield, Massachusetts in 1917, and died in 1985. She received an A.B. from Brenau College, and later was a graduate student at Williams College. In 1953 she married Charles Compton, a member of the Faculty. She had a great interest in literature, was broadly talented in business management and athletics, and had an extensive career in publishing, principally at the University of Chicago Press and Time, Inc.

8310

NORMANDALE COMMUNITY COLLEGE
LIBRARY
9700 FRANCE AVENUE SOUTH
BLOOMINGTON, MN 55431-4399